D0535944

LIFEWAYS

The Tlingit

RAYMOND BIAL

BENCHMARK BOOKS

MARSHALL CAVENDISH
NEW YORK

SERIES CONSULTANT: JOHN BIERHORST

ACKNOWLEDGMENTS

The Tlingit would not have been possible without the kind and generous assistance of several individuals and organizations. I would like to especially thank Saxman Native Village and Totem Bight State Historic Park, both located near Ketchikan, Alaska, for allowing me to make photographs at their outstanding sites. I would like to express my appreciation to Cheryl and John Katzeek of Keet Gooshi Tours who arranged a visit to Klukwan Village near Haines, Alaska. I would also like to thank Jerrie Clarke, curator at the Sheldon Museum and Cultural Center in Haines, who allowed me to photograph some of the impressive works of art in the collections. I would also like to acknowledge the other wonderful people whom we met during our travels, especially Nathan P. Jackson, Norman Nelson, Wayne Price, and Lee Wallace. Rain or shine, they brightened every day of our family's trip to southeastern Alaska.

I would like to thank my editors Kate Nunn and Christina Gardeski for their many helpful comments on this manuscript. I am once again indebted to John Bierhorst for his superb critical review of my efforts. As always, I offer my fondest appreciation for my wife Linda and my children Anna, Sarah, and Luke who joined me on our memorable journey through the Inside Passage of Alaska to visit the Tlingit and make the photographs for this book.

Benchmark Books
Marshall Cavendish
99 White Plains Road, Tarrytown, New York 10591-9001
Text copyright © 2003 by Raymond Bial
Map copyright © 2003 by the Marshall Cavendish Corporation
Map by Rodica Prato

All rights reserved. No part of this book may be reproduced in any form without
written permission from the publisher.

Library of Congress Cataloging-in-Publication Data
Bial, Raymond.
The Tlingit / by Raymond Bial.
p. cm. — (Lifeways)
Summary: Discusses the history, culture, social structure, beliefs, and notable people of the Tlingit.
Includes bibliographical references and index.
ISBN 0-7614-1414-2
1. Tlingit Indians—History—Juvenile literature. 2. Tlingit Indians—
Social life and customs—Juvenile literature. I. Title. II. Series.
E99.T6 B53 2002
979.8004'972—dc21
2001005941
Printed in Italy
6 5 4 3 2 1

Photo Research by Anne Burns Images

Cover Photos by Raymond Bial

The photographs in this book are used by permission and through the courtesy of: *American Museum of Natural History: Dept. of Library Sciences:* title page—neg.no.124885, p.28 neg.no.2A5148, p.30 neg.no.124890 copied by Morton Youvow; p.25 neg.no.338436, p.77 neg.no.41618 G.T.Emmons, 1888; p.40 neg.no.337541 copied by P.Hollenbeak/O.Bauer; p.44 neg.no.11213; p.46 neg.no.2A5147; p.50 neg.no.13989, p.55 neg.no.13991, p.67 neg.no.13986, p.72 neg.no.13973 copied by Thomas Lunt; p.79 neg.no.328740 E.W.Merrill. *Raymond Bial:* 6, 8–9, 13, 17, 18, 20, 22–23, 27, 33, 34, 36–37, 42, 48, 52, 56, 59, 60, 62, 64, 66, 69, 71, 74–75, 87, 91, 94, 97, 98, 99, 100–101, 105, 106–107. *National Museum of the American Indian:* 88–89, 92. *William Demmert:* 102, 111. *Alaska State Library:* p.113 01-3294 CORE. *Rosita Worl:* p.115.

This book is respectfully dedicated to the Tlingit, who flourish along the coastal waters of southeastern Alaska.

Contents

Author's Note

At THE DAWN OF THE TWENTIETH CENTURY, NATIVE Americans were thought to be a vanishing race. However, despite four hundred years of warfare, deprivation, and disease, American Indians have not gone away. Countless thousands have lost their lives, but over the course of this century the populations of native tribes have grown tremendously. Even as American Indians struggle to adapt to modern Western life, they have also kept the flame of their traditions alive—the language, religion, stories, and the everyday ways of life. An exhilarating renaissance in Native American culture is now sweeping the nation from coast to coast.

The Lifeways books depict the social and cultural life of the major nations, from the early history of native peoples in North America to their present-day struggles for survival and dignity. Historical and contemporary photographs of traditional subjects, as well as period illustrations, are blended throughout each book so that readers may gain a sense of family life in a tipi, a hogan, or a longhouse.

No single book can comprehensively portray the intricate and varied lifeways of an entire tribe, or nation. I only hope that young people will come away with a deeper appreciation for the rich tapestry of Indian culture—both then and now—and a keen desire to learn more about these first Americans.

1. Origins

Silhouetted against the setting sun, trees cling to the rocky shores of southeastern Alaska.

NO ONE KNOWS WHEN THE TLINGIT (TLING-GIT) FIRST SETTLED ALONG the coast of southeastern Alaska. According to some stories, they journeyed there from the headwaters of the Nass River countless generations ago. This region of British Columbia, just outside of the Tlingit territory, figures prominently in many of their origin stories. One tale recounts the activities of a great bird, *Raven*, at the source of the Nass River. Revered among the Tlingit, Raven could be a trickster, but he often helped people, as illustrated in the following story:

Raven Brings Light to the World

No one knows just how the story of Raven began, only that the mischievous trickster has always existed. He was even here long ago, when there was no light in the world. At that time, a rich man kept the light to himself in a large clan house far up the Nass River.

Raven was very clever and he wondered what he could do to bring light to the world. He finally came up with a plan. He made himself very small—as tiny as a speck of dust—and dropped into a stream near the man's home. The man's daughter drank from the stream, and magically she became heavy with child.

The rich man wondered how his daughter had become pregnant, yet he was overjoyed that he would soon have a grandchild. When the daughter went into labor, she lay down in a bed of plush furs. But the baby refused to be born on such finery. So, the people in the clan house spread moss to make a humble bed, and there the infant was born. His eyes were very bright as he glanced around.

The child grew rapidly and soon began to crawl around the clan house. The wealthy man was so pleased to have a grandson he did not question why the child was growing so fast.

One day, the child noticed three bentwood boxes of varying sizes and shapes hanging upon the walls. Pointing to the wooden boxes, the child wailed day after day. At last, the grandfather said to his daughter, "Give my grandson the box hanging on the end. That is the box of stars."

The box was taken down and given to the child who played happily. Rolling the box on the floor, he gradually moved toward the center of the clan house until he was under the smoke hole. Suddenly, he opened the box, releasing the stars, which rose through the smoke hole and ascended into the night sky. The stars quickly scattered throughout the heavens, just as they are today.

Some days later, the child began to cry with such anguish that people thought that he might die. The grandfather finally said to his daughter, "Untie the next box and give it to him."

The child played with the box under the smoke hole. After a while he opened the box and the moon floated up through the smoke hole, high into the sky.

Just one bentwood box remained—the one that held sunlight. The child now cried for this box. As he glanced around the clan house, his eyes changed colors and people began to suspect that he was not an ordinary little boy.

Yet a grandfather loves his grandchild as much as he does his own daughter. So, the grandfather said to his daughter, "Give it to him."

When the child had the box in his hands, he uttered the raven cry, "Ka!" and flew up through the smoke hole, carrying the sun with him. The world was suddenly flooded with light.

The rich man realized that Raven had only pretended to be his grandson. He shouted, "Raven has tricked me. He has taken all of my things."

And that is how Raven brought the light of the stars, moon, and sun into the world.

Early History

Like other Native Americans, the Tlingit originally migrated from Asia across a land bridge where the Bering Sea is today. It is believed that some Tlingit, whose original name means "human beings" or "people of the tidelands," have inhabited the shores and interior of southeastern Alaska for thousands of years. People entered the territory of the Tlingit at least ten thousand years ago. About five thousand years ago, these people began to settle in the coastal region. Most probably came from the south, some as recently as eight hundred years ago. The Tlingit possibly came from camps on the Nass, Skeena, Stikine, and Taku Rivers. They tended to move from south to north and from the coast to the interior, with some families moving upstream as well. In the eighteenth century, large numbers of Haida also pushed into the region and displaced many southern Tlingit people. The earliest known Tlingit villages date from A.D. 1200 to 1700. However, these settlements vanished, according to Tlingit stories, when they were destroyed by glaciers in the seventeenth and eighteenth century. It is

*G*laciers, such as the Mendenhall Glacier near present-day Juneau, slowly grind down passages between the mountains.

Tlingit Traditional Territory

Yakutat

Dry Bay

Chilkat

Chilkoot

Hoonah

Auk

Taku

PACIFIC

OCEAN

Hutsnuwu

Sumdum

Sitka

Kake

Kuiu

Stikine

Henya

Sanya

Klawock

Tongass

For many generations, the Tlingit have prospered on the coast and the islands of southeastern Alaska.

believed that some Tlingit also migrated from the interior when glaciers began to nearly block the rivers. These travelers had to pass under massive ice bridges that have since melted away.

The Tlingit have long fascinated visitors to their territory—from the first Russian adventurers of 1741 to present-day anthropologists. Early explorers found a complex society, rich in art and elaborate tradition, unlike that of other native people living on the coast. Unrelated to any of the tribes around them, the Tlingit spoke a language that was only vaguely similar to that of Athapaskan-speaking peoples who had long dominated the interior regions of Alaska and western Canada. The Tlingit also shared a few customs with Athapaskan peoples, having traded with them for centuries. The Tlingit and the Haida were often thought to be related. But the Haida only moved into the region from the Queen Charlotte Islands about two hundred years ago.

The Tlingit were composed of three principal groups: Gulf Coast, Northern, and Southern. These three groups all shared a common language and customs. The Gulf Coast Tlingit included the Hoonah of Lituya Bay; the Dry Bay Tlingit at the mouth of the Alsek River; and the Yakutat, who included Tlingit-speaking Eyak people from the Italio River to Icy Bay. In 1910 the Yakutat and Dry Bay Tlingit united as a people. The Northern Tlingit included the Hoonah on the north shore of Cross Sound, Chilkat, Chilkoot, Auk, and Taku; the Sumdum on the mainland; and the Sitka and Hutsnuwu, or Angoon, on the outer islands and coast. The Southern Tlingit were composed of the Kake, Kuiu, Henya, and Klawock on the islands; the Stikine, or Wrangell; the Tongass; and the Sanya, or Cape Fox, who lived on the mainland or coastal harbors. In addition there is a small group of Tlingit-speaking people living in inland British Columbia and adjacent Yukon Territory whose culture is partly Tlingit and partly Athapaskan. This book is mainly about the Tlingit proper, sometimes called Coastal Tlingit to distinguish themselves from these Inland Tlingit, who are believed to have had Athapaskan ancestors.

Tlingit neighbors to the south were the Tsimshian, while the Haida lived to the southeast, and various Athapaskan groups inhabited the interior on the east. To the north lived the Eyak, a coastal people whose language belonged to the Athapaskan family. As mentioned above, some of the Eyak people became Tlingit speakers and united with the Yakutat, the northernmost of the Tlingit groups.

The People and the Land

The Tlingit have long made their home on a narrow strip of land, known as the Alaskan panhandle, which stretches from Icy Bay in the north to Chatham Strait in the south. The land varies from misty tide-water to lofty, snowcapped mountains. At the northern end of Tlingit territory, along the Gulf of Alaska coast, there are few bays and other sheltered places for landing canoes. But to the south, an archipelago of windswept islands, just thirty miles wide and five hundred miles long, protects most of the shoreline from the battering waves of the ocean. It is a region of rolling waves, mountainous islands, and rugged coastline shaped long ago by numerous glaciers and fjords. Several rivers, notably the Stikine, Taku, Chilkat, and Alsek, cut

*W*ater tumbles, cold and clear, down the numerous streams that lace the mountainous region where the Tlingit have long made their home.

A colony of sea lions lounges on the rocks of an archipelago where the
Tlingit hunt and fish.

through the jagged mountains, providing water routes to the interior.

Thrust upward by the continental plates, the rocky land is blanketed in the north with lush rain forests of spruce, hemlock, and yellow cedar trees, and in the south with red cedar. These forests tower over a dense, tangled undergrowth abounding in blueberries. There are few temperature extremes; both winters and summers are relatively mild. Clouds often hang over the treetops, rain descends like a veil, and fog drifts low over the waters. The coast is drenched in rain for 200 to 260 days a year with total rainfall ranging from 100 to 220 inches, making the region the wettest in North America. During late autumn and winter, strong winds and snow occasionally swirl into the river valleys and blast the interior.

The waters of the Pacific Ocean teemed with sea mammals—harbor seals, fur seals, and sea otters, along with whales and porpoises. Traditionally, the Tlingit caught an abundance of fish, especially halibut, salmon, and herring. In early spring, people caught candlefish, also known as eulachon or hooligan.

As the weather warmed, the salmon began to run. The Tlingit caught five different kinds of salmon from midsummer until late autumn, when the rivers began to freeze over. Most of the salmon were dried and stored for the long, lean months of winter. At low tide the Tlingit gathered shellfish and seaweed that had washed onto the beach. During the spring and summer, ducks and other waterfowl migrated up the Pacific flyway. They nested or paused in the region, providing the Tlingit with eggs and meat. For fur and flesh, the Tlingit hunted a variety of wild animals—wolves, moose, black-tailed

An evergreen forest grows along the banks of a salmon river in view of snow-capped mountains.

deer, Dall sheep, and mountain goats. There were also marten, beaver, and mink. Black bears and grizzlies ranged throughout the ancestral Tlingit territory. The grizzlies along the coastal rivers became huge as they feasted on salmon while smaller grizzlies fed on plants and animals farther inland.

The Tlingit have long looked to the land and the water to provide themselves with food and the materials with which they made their clothing, belongings, and works of art. In the forests, they cut towering red cedar trees into logs from which they carved impressive totem poles. They also formed posts, beams, and wide planks for building their clan houses. They shaped the boards into bentwood boxes, crafted graceful canoes, and made other essential tools.

Because of the rugged terrain, people usually traveled by water among the scattered islands. Long before the arrival of Europeans, they paddled canoes, often for hundreds of miles, to wage war on enemies, trade with allies, and visit neighbors for lavish ceremonies known as potlatches.

2. A Home on Land and Sea

Carved and painted totem poles are positioned in front of this Tlingit house built near the present-day city of Ketchikan.

THE TLINGIT LIVED IN GROUPS OR VILLAGES KNOWN AS *KWAN*. THE PEOPLE in each kwan made their homes in the same geographic region, where they intermarried and lived peacefully with each other. There may have been fifteen to twenty kwan when the Tlingit first encountered European explorers. Communities where many Tlingit gathered had often "kwan" in the name—Sitka-kwan, Taku-kwan, Heeny-kwan, and so forth. Today, Ketchikan, Juneau, Wrangell, and other cities of southeastern Alaska are located on the village sites of several traditional kwan.

In each kwan's region, there was at least one main village, often situated on a sheltered cove. It was ideally located near hunting grounds, berry patches, clam beds, deep water for halibut, and other food sources. The village had to be near fresh water, stands of timber, and trails or streams that led into the interior. If the community was also located near a salmon river, the people might live there year-round. However, most Tlingit lived in the village only during the winter, then abandoned it in the summer for fishing and hunting camps. As cold weather set in, they returned to the winter village.

The village consisted of a row of large plank houses facing the beach. People often built palisades around their houses or occasionally around the entire village. Sometimes, wealthy nobles constructed a fort nearby where they could defend themselves against invaders. Canoes were usually pushed up onto the beach in front of the house and kept under mats or shelters. Throughout the village stood smokehouses and drying racks for preserving fish. Small houses on poles and plank-lined

*I*n this 1888 photograph, a Tlingit woman dries strips of halibut and salmon in the summer village of Hoonah at Glacier Bay.

pits were used for storing food and belongings. There were also sweat huts and shelters used by the women during menstruation and childbirth. Boxes holding the powerful and sacred objects of the shaman, or medicine man, were hidden in the nearby forest, well away from the people in the village.

Clan Houses

Large rectangular houses served as both homes and ceremonial buildings. About six families, totaling forty to fifty people, including slaves, lived in each clan house. Four corner posts, elaborately carved and painted with ancestral and totem designs, formed the basic structure and a ridge beam supported the gently-sloping, peaked roof. Thick, wide cedar planks were used to sheath the walls and gabled roof of the clan house. There were no windows in the building—only a small oval doorway. Through openings in the roof light streamed into the plank house and smoke from cooking fires drifted upward into the sky.

Inside, the earthen floor was dug slightly lower to make two or three levels. The nobles who owned the clan house required their slaves to sleep on the ground by the oval doorway. Commoners who were related to the nobles or worked for them slept on benches or platforms on one of the lower levels where they tended their own fires for warmth and cooking. In the middle of the clan house there was a large communal hearth where meals were cooked for the nobles and their guests at celebrations. On the highest level at the back of the clan house, the nobles occupied secluded rooms where they slept on wooden platforms. Their small apartments were separated with mats, piles of boxes, or wooden screens carved and painted with clan crests. These partitions could be removed to make a large space for ceremonies. Valuable treasures were also hidden away in this space. A platform in front of these rooms was known as the "head of house," or place of honor where the owner and his family sat, guests were received, and the deceased might lie in state. The oldest man of the

Light streams through the smoke hole, illuminating the plank walls, timbers, and totem poles within this clan house.

*T*his house, belonging to members of the Killer Whale clan, illustrates how Tlingit homes were adorned with traditional designs into the 1950s and later.

noble family was usually considered the owner and chief, but his mother and sisters were highly influential members of the household as well.

In the late nineteenth century, carpentry tools, nails, and sawn lumber became available to the Tlingit. Many people who had become wealthy through fishing began to build large frame houses on pilings with modern windows, doors, and iron stoves. Several families lived in each of these houses that they furnished with brass beds, tables, and chairs. Later, the houses were divided into separate, unheated rooms, but people complained that these dwellings were not as warm as the old clan houses. People displayed painted crests on these houses. However, by the 1920s, an influential organization known as the Alaska Native Brotherhood had convinced many people to do away with this practice. Many people are now returning to the traditions of their ancestors, including the painting of crests on their homes.

Tlingit Society

The Tlingit believed, and continue to believe, that every individual belongs to one of two moieties, or separate halves: Raven and Wolf (sometimes called Eagle in the north). The two moieties were opposites in every aspect of life, including marriage, death, and important ceremonies. Among the Tlingit, everything in daily life and the universe was ordered around the moieties and their relations with each other. Each moiety comprised more than thirty clans, which were further divided into family lineages, or house groups of related families, descending from a common ancestor. Members of clans in one moiety had to marry into clans of the other moiety. One could not marry a member of one's own moiety. A Wolf had to marry a Raven, and a Raven had to marry a Wolf.

This family gathered at their summer fishing house on Georges Island at Cross Sound in 1888.

Tlingit society was also matrilineal, which means children traced their descent through the mother's side of the family. Children were always considered part of their mother's family. Throughout life, the mother's brothers played more crucial roles than the father in raising the children because they were more closely related to their sister than her husband. A man also inherited wealth and his social position through his mother's side of the family. Titles, crests, and other privileges were considered hereditary property as well.

The complex society was also hierarchical, with individuals and lineages ranked from commoners to nobility. Upper classes, or nobles, owned the largest houses and enjoyed the greatest wealth and prominence, along with the rights to hunt and gather near the villages. Commoners had to pay to hunt, fish, or gather in these places. Commoners achieved some respect as artists, such as mask or canoe makers. They could also achieve higher status by becoming shamans. Others were simply considered the lower classes. Many Tlingit owned slaves, who were captives and their children seized in battles with neighboring tribes. Slaves had no rights and were not regarded as part of Tlingit society. They were forced to do the hardest chores around the village. Yet if they proved themselves as craftsmen, hunters, and fishermen they might someday be freed and respected for their ability. After the United States acquired Alaska in 1867, slaves were liberated and became the lowest members of the social order.

The noble members of a particular clan or family lineage held all territory and property rights including rights to locations for houses, graves, and camps for fishing, hunting, berry picking, and gathering seaweed. All clan property could be sold, traded, or given away, usually when an owner died, or taken in warfare. Clan and lineage chiefs, or headmen, managed the wealth of their group and directed hunting and fishing activities. They also ordered the death of trespassers and hosted memorial services.

The law was based upon moiety, clan, and house. Any injury to members on the other side had to be resolved by payment of goods, property, or services. If a commoner murdered a chief and could not come up with adequate payment, the chief of his clan might be killed. Occasionally, hostages known as "deer" were exchanged for a period of eight days as proof of earnest intent to settle a dispute peacefully. The "deer" rested quietly, enjoying good food and comforts, as the negotiations were underway. In the case of major disputes, such as a war, a clan might have to give a valuable crest to its opponent.

The Tlingit went to war against other clans or tribes for plunder or revenge. They not only killed their enemies, but captured women and children as slaves. Their weapons included bows and arrows, spears, war clubs, and knives. Warriors protected themselves with armor made of hides and wooden rods worn over moose-skin shirts. Upon their return, they celebrated a victory with feasting and dancing.

Along with personal wealth, each clan owned certain emblems, or pictorial designs, known as "crests." The clan's crest represented its totem, which was usually an animal but might be a heavenly body, a

Clan members often painted crests, such as the proud and powerful eagle, on their houses and musical instruments.

natural feature such as the ocean, or a supernatural being like the thunderbird. Each clan inherited these crests. Many crests were over a thousand years old. Crests honored ancestors and granted special rights to clan members. For example, in one well-known story of Glacier Bay, a careless girl triggered a glacier that destroyed much of her

*T*lingit carvers devoted themselves to creating works of art, including these elaborate totem poles standing at the forest's edge.

town and her grandmother had to pay with her own life. Descendants in their clan have since used glacier as a crest symbol.

The major Raven crest symbols were Raven, Owl, Whale, Sea Lion, Salmon, Frog, Sleep Bird, Big Dipper, Sun, Moon, and Ocean. Those of the Wolf, or Eagle, were Wolf, Eagle, Petrel, Bear, Killer Whale, Shark, Halibut, Thunderbird, and others. Crests were prominently featured on canoes, feast dishes, clothing, blankets, drums, rattles, and other cherished objects. People also proudly displayed their crests on totem poles and the house posts that supported the entrance wall of the dwelling. A Tlingit noble who wished to make known his deeds or those of his ancestors carefully selected crest designs. He then hired an artist who beautifully carved and painted the pole in a style in which a curving black frame outlined each sculpted figure. A totem pole could be placed at the entrance to the noble's home, used to honor the remains of a deceased relative, or raised as a memorial on the beach. When the totem pole was finished, a celebration called a potlatch was held. The guests helped to raise the pole, after which everyone enjoyed a great feast and told many stories about the figures depicted on the towering pole.

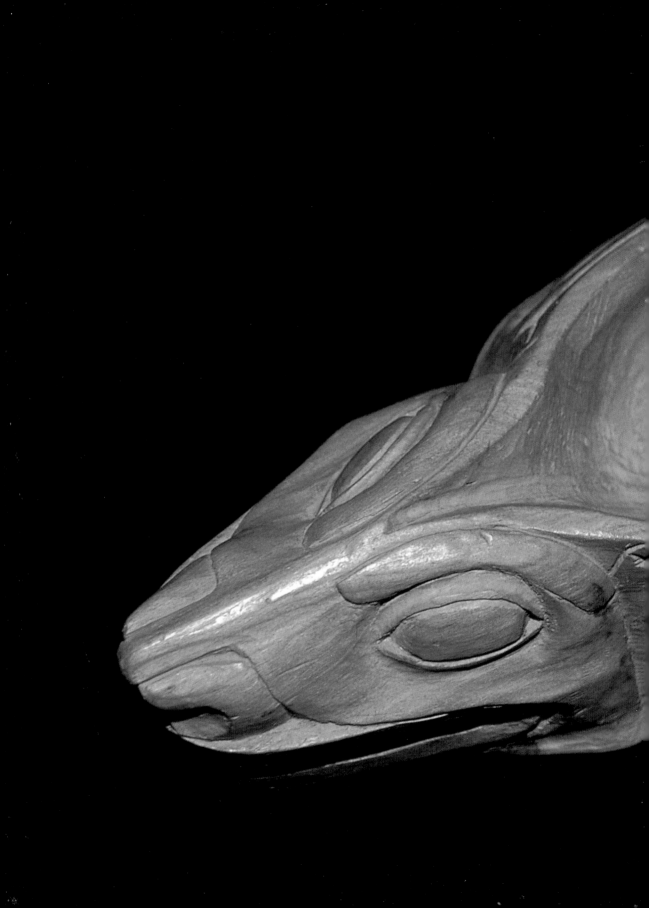

3. Lifeways

The Tlingit excelled
in carving useful
objects, such as this
potlatch bowl.

THE TLINGIT LIVED ACCORDING TO THE SEASONS. DURING THE SPRING, people hunted on the mainland, fished for halibut in the deep waters of the sea, caught shellfish, and gathered seaweed. As the days warmed, they hunted seals. Then throughout the summer and into the fall, they caught salmon during the several runs. They also hunted sea otters and dug wild potatoes in the fall. In November, as cold weather approached, they settled in their winter villages. Through the long, dark winter, they held potlatches and traded. Each family followed similar cycles from one generation to the next.

Cycle of Life

Birth. The Tlingit thought that infants were the reincarnation of relatives on the mother's side of the family who would carry on the name of her family lineage and clan. They believed that babies often remembered people and events from their previous life. Between death and rebirth, one "was ashes." The Tlingit regarded a person as a number of layers around a core of mind, soul, and emotions. The outer body had eight parts, counted by doubling the number of upper and lower limbs—four for the arms and four for the legs.

When a woman was about to give birth, she was accompanied to a bark shelter by two or more experienced women, often her husband's sisters, who helped to deliver the baby. They were later paid well for their assistance. The mother and her newborn remained in the shelter for about ten days to avoid contaminating the clan house and its inhabitants.

Childhood. When a boy turned seven or eight years old, he went to live with one of his mother's brothers to begin his education. The uncle taught the young man about his family heritage and his responsibilities to his clan and lineage—especially if the uncle was a house owner or chief and the boy was his heir. Under his uncle's guidance, the boy toughened and purified himself by plunging into icy water in the morning, whipping his own body, chopping piles of firewood, and undertaking other vigorous tasks. From his uncle, the boy learned the many rituals and beliefs, as well as the practical skills, involved in fishing and hunting. Until he killed his first game, a young man could eat only certain foods. He came of age when he brought home his prey. A great feast was then held in his honor, after which he was regarded as a "master of game."

Mothers took primary responsibility for educating and training their daughters. They instructed them in their important roles in their families and the community. Tlingit women generally enjoyed high status, mostly because they were responsible for the arduous work of drying and smoking the fish that sustained everyone in the village. So, it was essential that a mother properly teach her daughter the many skills and tasks that she would need to provide for her family and manage a household. These included cooking meals, making clothing, and caring for the children. Until she had her first period, a girl also had to abstain from certain foods, a practice through which she learned the importance of sacrifice and discipline.

Dressed in ceremonial garments, including a headband and nose ring, this young boy prepares for a dance.

Coming-of-Age. A girl came of age when she had her first period. At this time she was confined in a dark room or cellar in the clan house for at least eight days, but often much longer, depending on her rank and wealth. A high-ranking girl might be secluded for two years. During the girl's seclusion, her father's sister, who represented his lineage, closely supervised her, while her mother and grandmother instructed her in the traditions of their house.

During her seclusion the young woman also performed many rituals and observed many restrictions to assure prosperity in the future. For example, to avoid contaminating herself, she could touch herself only with a scratcher. She washed her hair in blackberry juice and wore a black feather cap believing that her hair would keep its dark color in old age. For the first eight days of seclusion, she ate and drank nothing, except a little water on the fourth and eighth day. If she reached eagerly for the drink, it was thrown away, so that she would learn self-control. At the end of her eight-day fast, her maternal relatives held a feast. At this time her dolls were given away to paternal cousins. During the remainder of her two-year seclusion, the young woman was not allowed to eat fresh fish, shellfish, or seaweed. She ate only from her own dishes. If she glanced at the sky, it was believed that there would be storms, so she had to wear a hood draped with strings of dentalia shells.

At the end of her seclusion, the young woman was bathed and then dressed in new clothes. She was adorned with gold bracelets and other jewelry. She emerged from the room or cellar with a pale complexion that was much admired. However, because of her inac-

Girls liked to play with dolls representing the native peoples of Alaska, including the Tlingit.

tivity, her legs had become so weak that she could barely stand or walk more than a few steps. Her lower lip was pierced for a piece of jewelry known as a labret. Families of high status also gave a potlatch to thank her paternal aunts for their devoted efforts. These aunts then presented the young woman as ready to be married.

Marriage. Any man and woman of opposite moieties could marry each other, but in high-ranking families marriages were often arranged. Ideally, couples were of equal rank so that their marriage would strengthen the bonds between houses and clans. Marriages of nobles, in particular, served to build and maintain alliances between families.

During the marriage ceremony, the fathers of the young man and woman exchanged gifts, often valuable crest objects. Some marriages were arranged to obtain such wealth. A rich man whose gifts were accepted then took his bride home. However, a common man unable to provide sufficient gifts had to remain in the home of the bride and work for the father-in-law as a form of payment, or "bride price."

A man might be married to two or more sisters at the same time. If his wife died, he was entitled to marry her younger sister or another close relative. Few women had more than one husband, but a widow was expected to marry her husband's brother or maternal nephew. Although these marriages united families and clans, they often matched couples of very unequal age. When a young man or woman had to take a much older person as a mate, a related young person was also designated as "future wife" or "future husband" to take the place of the older spouse upon his or her death.

Death. When a man, woman, or child died, the rites varied widely according to the rank and lineage of the deceased. There was an elaborate ceremony when a noble or house or clan chief passed away. A lavish funeral ended with a great memorial potlatch in which the successor inherited his wealth and position. When a shaman died, special rituals were observed. The widow and mourners did not cut their hair, and his body was not cremated. It was placed in a small house or cave,

*A*s he lay dying, this Tlingit chief was surrounded by his wealth, consisting of
countless carved wooden objects and blankets.

along with some of his sacred objects and the image of a spirit
guardian. In contrast, the bodies of slaves were thrown onto the beach
to be washed away in the sea or devoured by scavengers.

When a nobleman died there were usually eight days of
mourning. Clan members gathered to sing four mourning songs and
make donations to pay for the funeral. Men of the opposite moiety,
especially those married to the deceased's sisters, prepared the body

and made all the arrangements, including the wake and cremation. Similarly, the body of a deceased woman was attended by her husband's sisters. With his body adorned in ceremonial clothes and his face painted with clan designs, the deceased was propped up at the head of the house, with his wealth piled around him.

The wake continued for eight days, although the time might be longer for a chief. Mourners wore old clothes with ropes tied around their waists. They cut their hair or later burned it at the cremation. Widows observed especially harsh rituals, such as fasting, to express their grief. After four days, the body was taken out of the house through an opening made by removing a plank from the wall. It was carried to a pyre and cremated while mourners sang four more songs and the women of the widow's family, wrapped in button blankets, swayed to the music. Valuables of the deceased were thrown into the fire. It was believed that burning the body released the soul which then departed the village through the forest before climbing a mountain to "the other side." Afterward, members of the opposite clan gathered the ashes and bones in a blanket and placed them in a grave box or mortuary totem pole.

After the funeral, the widow and other mourners bathed and put on new clothing. They burned all their old garments. That evening the mourners held a potlatch for the opposite moiety to show their gratitude. The widow or widower was expected to remarry a member of that house or clan after a year of mourning.

To honor the deceased, many Tlingit, especially those living in the south, traditionally raised tall carved and painted mortuary poles near their homes. Those living in the north tended to keep the ashes in boxes painted with clan crests or covered with a valuable Chilkat blanket and placed high on poles. Over time, the Tlingit did not raise these grave boxes. In the late nineteenth century, through Christian influence, the Tlingit began to bury their dead. They built a small house on the grave with doors and glass windows through which one could view the cherished belongings of the deceased. Over time, the houses were replaced by cement slabs and the graves were often fenced. The Tlingit also came to use marble tombstones on which crest symbols were carved. In recent years, they have added Christian inscriptions and images.

At a chief's funeral, a Chilkat blanket was placed above the burial box that sheltered his remains.

Hunting, Fishing, and Gathering

The Tlingit fished and hunted for survival, yet they also believed that every creature had a soul. No animal, not even the smallest bird, was killed needlessly or wasted. Instead of attempting to dominate the wilderness, a hunter respected his prey. Before a hunt, he observed a number of strict rituals. He purified himself by fasting and bathing. He did not speak of the game he sought, especially bears since it was thought that these powerful animals could hear what was said of them. His wife and children also had to remain silent until his return, because any inappropriate utterance or action might influence the hunt, change the weather, or bring misfortune, even death. The hunter also relied on magical amulets. He departed before dawn and fasted during his pursuit of game. He might carry a dried salmon in the event of an emergency, but it was generally believed that he would hunt better if the animals knew that he was hungry. After he made a kill, he prayed to the dead body and spirit of the animal. He explained his need for its flesh and begged to be forgiven. Raising his voice in song, he thanked the animal for having given its life. He might also make an offering of eagle down. He returned the vital parts, such as the head, bones, and certain organs to the water, or burned them, to ensure that the animal would be reincarnated.

Men hunted many kinds of land animals, often with the help of dogs. Bears were trapped in deadfalls and snares, shot with bows and arrows, or most often with spears. For hunting and for warfare men made six- to eight-foot spears of spruce or hemlock shafts. Most

*P*erched high on a branch overlooking the water, the bald eagle continues to be a powerful symbol of the Tlingit.

often, hunters pursued bears in the early spring when their fur was in prime condition for making robes. Three or four dogs either roused a bear from a den or tracked and held the animal at bay until the hunters arrived for the kill. For hunting deer, mountain goats, Dall sheep, and other animals, men used bows of yew or hemlock and arrows of yellow cedar. Spears and arrows were fitted with a sharp blade of slate, copper and, in later years, iron. In ancient times, men also hunted with whip slings and darts. Young men ventured above the timberline to hunt deer while older men ordered their well-trained dogs to chase the fleet-footed animals down to the shore where they could be shot from canoes. Dogs also drove mountain goats and Dall sheep to the hunters. They killed these animals for their fat, their horns, which were used to make spoons and feast dishes, and their wool which was woven into clothing. Tlingit people who lived inland hunted caribou, moose, and occasionally wood bison.

The Tlingit speared or netted beaver under the ice. They caught ducks, geese, and other waterfowl, often with skillfully placed snares. These birds were sought not only for their succulent meat, but for their feathers and beaks, which were used to adorn clothing. However, they never hunted land otters. It was believed that people who had drowned or died in the woods were reincarnated as these animals. It was also believed that when a shaman died his spirit most often assumed the form of a land otter.

The Tlingit relied heavily on fish as a source of food, especially on five kinds of salmon—king (chinook), pink (humpback), silver

*N*ear their summer village, these Tlingit people are fishing from handmade boats in the Chilkat River.

(coho), red (sockeye), and chum (dog salmon). In late spring, they moved to their fishing camps where they remained until fall, except for some winter villages that were already located on salmon rivers. Some of the fish were boiled, baked, or roasted. However, the women helped by slaves sun-dried or cured the salmon in smokehouses, and then wrapped most of the fish in bales for the winter. Salmon caught late in the season was often frozen whole during the cold weather.

The Tlingit employed a variety of clever methods for harvesting salmon. Most were caught in boxlike traps made of wooden slats placed across an opening in a weir. People living on the Chilkat River also used funnel-shaped traps for salmon and eulachon. On tidal streams, men sometimes made stone walls on which they piled branches. When the tide fell, salmon became trapped and were easily caught. In August, when water levels became low, the Tlingit placed a row of sharp stakes across the mouth of a river. As they tried to swim upstream, the salmon impaled themselves on the stakes and were gathered. The Tlingit also caught salmon with harpoons or spears fitted with barbed points of antler, bone or copper—the same kind they used to kill seals, sea lions, sea otters, and porpoises.

In the rivers and sea around them, the Tlingit caught trout, cod, rock cod, herring, and halibut with hooks and lines made from animal gut. Some fishermen also trolled for salmon using herring as bait. To catch halibut in deep waters, they devised a large, ingenious fish hook of yellow cedar and alder wood with a sharp barb made of bone, and later of iron. They used a piece of octopus as bait, a stone

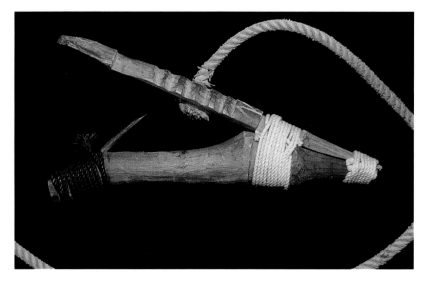

The Tlingit used large, hand-crafted fishhooks to catch halibut in deep ocean waters.

as a sinker, and an inflated seal stomach or a wood figure of a bird as a float. Halibut might weigh as much as one hundred pounds and fishermen faced a daunting task in hauling in a large, thrashing fish without capsizing their boat. To catch herring, a man standing in the bow of a canoe dragged a rake of thirty to fifty sharp bones or nails through the school of fish, impaling several fish at once. Herring were prized for their flesh and oil, but especially for their roe. Men also placed hemlock branches in shallow water where the herring spawned, then came back to collect their eggs. During spring and summer runs, they also caught candlefish in dip nets or in funnel traps. These small fish were valued for their delicious meat and rich oil. The fish had so much oil that people inserted a twisted spruce bark wick in them and burned the fish as candles.

The Tlingit depended on the ocean for many other foods. At low tide, they gathered seaweed and caught shellfish along the beach. They also hunted many kinds of sea mammals for their flesh and fur, notably harbor seals, fur seals, sea lions, sea otters, and porpoises. Unlike the Haida and other coastal tribes, they rarely hunted whales and only the bravest men attempted to kill a sea lion. Yet this animal's thick hide was valued for making heavy cords and ropes. Paddling along in their canoes, they most often speared otters and seals with harpoons. They rendered the seals' blubber into oil, ate the otters' meat, and fashioned the plush furs of both animals into warm clothing.

Women and children also gathered berries, such as blueberries, elderberries, wild strawberries, and highbush cranberries. These were eaten fresh or preserved by cooking and shaping into cakes that were dried or stored in wooden boxes filled with oil. The Tlingit also enjoyed the sweet inner bark of hemlock trees. During the early spring, they harvested the tender shoots of salmonberries, angelica, and cow parsnips. In spring and fall, they dug roots, especially fern, riceroot, and wild sweet potatoes.

Because of the rocky landscape and chilly weather, the Tlingit did not typically cultivate crops. However, in the early nineteenth century, people at Angoon and Killisnoo became well known for growing small potatoes, which they most likely acquired from the Russians who had settled there. At one time, the Tlingit also grew tobacco which was dried and mixed with yellow cedar ashes and lime from crushed and roasted seashells. Mixing the tobacco with spruce or cedar gum, they made pellets which were sucked for their flavor.

After the Russians introduced leaf tobacco and pipes, the Tlingit made ornately carved pipes, often with crest symbols, and smoked at funerals. Yet women still used tobacco pellets until around 1900.

Food Preparation

Fresh deer meat, especially the liver, was prized by the Tlingit. Meat was often slightly cooked or smoked, then preserved in oil or stored in a box with fat poured over the contents. Women skillfully cut salmon and halibut so thinly that the flesh could be easily dried, smoked, and tied into bundles. Salmon heads and eggs were fermented and eaten as a delicacy like rich cheese. The Tlingit also cooked salmon eggs, often with black seaweed or berries.

Oil was rendered from salmon heads, eulachon, herring, seal blubber, and mountain goat fat. Better grease was obtained from rancid fish and seal fat, so the fish were first left in a pit and blubber was kept in a sealskin bag for several days. To render fat, especially from candlefish, the Tlingit used a canoe as a large pot. They filled the canoe with water and fish, and brought the water to a boil by adding hot rocks. The oil was released from the fish into the water and was then strained into boxes. Any remaining oil was squeezed from the fish by hand or by sitting on them.

Kindling a fire with a red cedar hand drill or iron pyrite and quartz strikers, women baked foods in earthen ovens lined with leaves or boiled them in watertight boxes or baskets filled with heated rocks. They made spoons and dippers from hardwood or the horns of sheep and goats. They served food on wooden platters and dishes

*T*his man is using a large boat to render oil from candlefish that were caught nearby.

The Tlingit crafted bentwood boxes with rounded corners in which to store food and personal belongings.

with basketry cups and woven mats. Feast utensils were elaborately adorned with crest emblems and inlaid with abalone shell. Baskets, bags, and boxes were used for storage, the finest of which were bentwood boxes with tightly-fitting corners and lids, and spruce root baskets woven with striking geometric designs of dyed grass and fern stems.

The Tlingit have long relied on the land and the water to provide the food on which they sustain themselves. This modern recipe uses a favorite traditional food.

Fish Pie

Ingredients

Pastry:

2 cups all-purpose flour

$^1/_2$ cup vegetable oil

3 tablespoons cold water

Filling:

$^1/_2$ pound halibut, cut into 1-inch cubes

2 cups cooked rice

$^1/_2$ cup onions, chopped

2 hard-boiled eggs, chopped

$^1/_2$ teaspoon salt

$^1/_2$ teaspoon pepper

Directions

Preheat oven to 350 degrees. Add oil to flour and mix well with a fork. Sprinkle three tablespoons of cold water over pastry and mix well. Divide pastry in half and form into balls. Roll each ball into flat circles about eleven inches in diameter. Fit one circle of pastry dough into a pie pan and trim any excess from the edges. Spread one cup cooked rice in pie pan. Place halibut cubes on the rice, then layer with onions and eggs, followed by the second cup of rice. Cover with the other circle of dough, crimping along the edge.

Make several slits in the dough as steam vents. Bake thirty to thirty-five minutes or until the crust is golden brown.

You may substitute fresh or canned salmon for the halibut in this recipe.

Tlingit Carving

The Tlingit were highly skilled at many handicrafts, including beadwork and basketry. However, from ancient times to the present day, they have been most renowned as carvers. The striking, carved designs traditionally portrayed animals, either realistically or in a highly stylized form. Totem poles and many other carved objects were usually painted in the traditional blue-green and red colors of the Tlingit. Often, the animals' features, notably the eyes, fins, feathers, or joints, were traced by bold, curving black lines.

Talented artists made many kinds of objects, ranging in shape and size from amulets to totem poles. They carved goat and sheep horns into impressive feasting spoons. They hammered gold and silver coins, as well as native copper, into distinctive shapes that they then carved. Carvers emphasized objects that reflected deeply held beliefs and enhanced ceremonies. Masks, rattles, and staffs were carved and painted for potlatch dances and songs and for the healing rituals undertaken by shamans. Ornately carved bowls and eating utensils were displayed only at potlatches, while those for everyday meals were more simply adorned. Carvers made bentwood boxes for storing food and clothing as well. They also crafted water-tight boxes for cooking soups and stews. These boxes were not placed over a fire; instead hot stones were dropped into the boxes to bring the water to a boil. Large partition screens were exquisitely carved, often with a family crest.

Carvers worked with ivory, antler, and bone, but most often they worked with wood. Surrounded by lush rain forests, the Tlingit lived in the midst of an abundance of timber. For carving totem poles they

Among the most impressive Tlingit works of art are totem poles on which figures, such as this eagle, were carved and painted.

used red and yellow cedar. These woods have a straight grain, which splits evenly, making them excellent choices for clan house planks as well. Alder was traditionally preferred for dishes and eating utensils, since this wood does not affect the flavor of the food. Today, some carvers also work with birch, which has a lovely grain.

Carving tools included adzes, axes, drills, and knives. These tools and blades originally were made of stone, bone, or shell. In the late eighteenth century, the Tlingit began to forge iron tools. They acquired the metal through trade or salvaged iron from shipwrecks. Carvers turned the point of a drill to make a hole through which they sewed or tied pieces of wood together. They used many kinds of adzes to carefully shape pieces of wood. Sharp knives of many shapes and sizes were designed to snugly fit the hand of the carver, allowing him to give purposeful form to the wood.

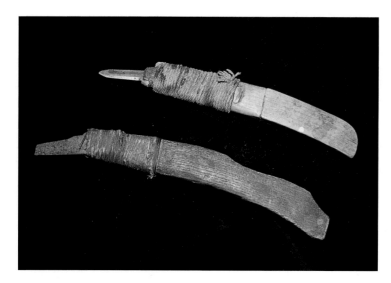

Carvers used sharp knives to shape wooden objects ranging in size from small bowls to towering totem poles.

Explorers on the Northwest coast were struck by the house posts and totem poles that towered over native villages like cedar monuments at the edge of the sea. Carved with figures of animals and people, some of these poles were ninety feet tall. Totems of animals such as a bear, eagle, or killer whale were carved in the wood and painted. Poles and posts exhibited family crests, related a story, recounted an event, or explained a tradition—one could actually read the pictorial language of the carving. Known as genealogy poles, they were usually placed in front of the owner's home. Anyone passing by immediately knew the clan of the mother of the house. Other poles related the history of the clan through stories. From the carving, anyone could learn about an episode in the mythical past of the family that had influenced the destiny of their ancestors. Perhaps their starving ancestors had once been aided by a creature or they had discovered fire. For example, the totem of the Kats house tells how Kats, a young warrior, ventured into the forest to stalk a grizzly bear. However, he fell in love with a female bear who appeared to him as a beautiful woman. His adventure became a story of love, death, and the revenge of the clan.

The Tlingit carved memorial poles to honor a chief or beloved relative who had died. The ashes of the deceased were placed in a special compartment in the back of the pole. Carvers also made poles to mark an important event such as the birth of a child or a courageous deed of a warrior. Significant historic events could be recognized on a totem pole. When the United States purchased Alaska in 1867, people learned of the Emancipation Proclamation, which had not only freed

This totem pole in Saxman Village near Ketchikan rises into the misty sky.

the Southern slaves but also ended slavery in Alaska. Chief Ebbits, whose family had lost its land and reputation on account of harboring escaped slaves from the Tlingit and Haida, erected an impressive pole in Lincoln's memory. Atop this 55-foot pole is a likeness of the bearded president in tall black hat and coat.

Carving was—and still is—both an expression of the Tlingit way of life and an art form. Today, the works of Tlingit artists are prized by collectors and museums throughout the world.

Clothing and Jewelry

During warm weather, men and women traditionally wore loin-cloths and skirts made of cedar bark. On rainy days, coastal people also put on waterproof basket caps made from twined spruce root and poncho-like raincoats made from spruce roots or cedar bark. Their clothing also included woven shirts, aprons, and leggings. They prominently displayed house and clan emblems on their clothing; the cone-shaped hats served as especially important crest objects. The Tlingit most likely learned the art of weaving from the Tsimshian.

As winter approached, people switched to warm clothing made of tanned animal skins and wrapped themselves in blankets woven from cedar bark, goat wool, or dog hair. People living in the interior wore leather pants with moccasins attached and shirts made of tanned caribou or moose hides. During the harsh winter, they favored goat wool pants, fur robes, and hooded sweaters made of caribou skins or hare pelts.

Chilkat blankets were the most impressive articles of clothing made by the Tlingit. In fact, Chilkat blankets were considered the most elaborate and highly valued textiles of any of the native peoples of the Northwest coast. The blankets served as robes in ceremonies in which the dances were regarded as complex expressions of art. Although named after the Chilkat tribe whose members came to excel at making the handicrafts, these blankets were originally woven

Making the highly valued Chilkat blankets requires considerable labor and talent.

by the Tsimshian. After they had mastered the craft Tlingit women typically devoted one to five years to weaving mountain goat wool and strips of cedar bark to make a single blanket. Each of the intricately woven blankets featured a distinctive emblem of the clan. Worn over the shoulders as a cape, Chilkat blankets were symbols of wealth and traditionally only clan leaders of great prestige could afford one. To give away a Chilkat blanket was a sign of great wealth, because only the very rich could afford to be so generous.

In the twentieth century, this art form was nearly lost as old weavers passed away. However, thanks to the dedicated efforts of several individuals, there are now many weavers, young and old, among the Tlingit and other coastal native groups, who are making Chilkat blankets and teaching the craft to others.

The complicated technique of weaving the garment known as Raven's Tail cape nearly vanished as well. These black and white capes with geometric and herringbone designs were not made for almost two centuries. Thanks to a cultural revival, the capes are now being woven throughout southeast Alaska. The techniques for making Chilkat blankets and Raven's Tail capes are also used to weave other dance regalia, including leggings, medicine bags, purses, aprons, tunics, and shirts.

Today, Tlingit regalia often features a dancing robe known as a button blanket. Although it takes a long time to make these beautiful and expensive blankets, they are still more readily available than either Chilkat blankets or Raven's Tail capes. The Tlingit first made button blankets when they acquired felt from Russian traders.

Wrapped in button blankets, these dancers pause briefly outside the clan house at Saxman Village.

Usually red, black, or blue, the blankets are adorned with house or clan crests outlined or solidly beaded with buttons made of a seashell called mother-of-pearl. Worn at gatherings, like Chilkat blankets, these robes are a means for people to display their family heritage.

During ceremonies men and women also wore headdresses. For men, these might be as simple as a headband or as elaborate as a hat carved from cedar wood. The clan crest was prominently featured on these hats, often trimmed with white ermine and inlaid with abalone shell. Women wore sailor-style hats modeled after those worn by Russian seamen. Made from the same felt as button blankets, these hats were adorned with beaded tassels.

To enhance their appearance, men and women also groomed their hair and adorned themselves with jewelry. They hung earrings from

In the early twentieth century, these Tlingit men posed in elaborately ornamented garments.

pierced ears and labrets from pierced noses. They wore bracelets and necklaces. They also painted their faces and tattooed their bodies. Many of these styles of dress and adornment, except for the labret, are still popular today. Through formal attire, the Tlingit continue not only to display their power, wealth, and heritage, but also to strengthen the social bonds within their community. In making and wearing a garment, they honor their ancestors and show respect toward other clans. The relationship of the garment maker and the wearer and of their respective clans is emphasized.

Travel and Trade

For the Tlingit, especially those living along the coast, canoes were the primary means of travel. The many styles included forked prow canoes, shallow river canoes, and ice-hunting canoes used in pursuing seals. Men also crafted small canoes with upturned ends to use when catching fish and hunting otter. Tlingit living inland sometimes paddled skin canoes, but most often they used small dugouts or rafts if they were not able to make their way on foot. On the coasts, the Tlingit constructed both large, oceangoing canoes, which could carry as many as sixty people, and small canoes, which men and women navigated down rivers and along the beach. Craftsmen usually made canoes during the winter months when they were not busy with hunting and fishing. Making a canoe required wisdom and great skill. Men first carefully selected the wood—cottonwood for a small canoe and red or yellow cedar for a large vessel. They preferred red cedar, but these trees grew mostly to the south in the territory of

The Tlingit made large, graceful canoes to travel to other villages and to fish.

the Haida. Tlingit living in this area often harvested red cedars, and other Tlingit sometimes traded with the Haida for red cedar logs.

To make a small canoe, men first hollowed out the log with an adze, then filled the vessel with water heated with hot rocks. The steam and hot water softened the wood which was then painstakingly shaped. The sides were gradually pulled and pushed apart and the ends were gracefully tapered. The canoe was then dried and smoked over a pitch fire to waterproof and blacken the wood. To make a large canoe, men skillfully hollowed out and joined separate logs to form a high prow and stem. The prow often featured carved figures and the finished canoe was painted with crests and other clan symbols. The men made brushes from bear or porcupine hair and applied a waterproof paint made by blending minerals, salmon eggs, and chewed spruce gum.

Over land and water, the Tlingit established and maintained a vast trade network. This network linked the Northwest coast with the Athapaskan peoples who lived inland to the east and north, the Inuit of the northern coast and Siberia, and several tribes to the south, especially the Tsimshian and Haida. Over the course of several generations, privileged Tlingit chiefs came to enjoy hereditary rights to trade with Athapaskan leaders. They even married high-ranking women of these tribes to strengthen these relations. Trade routes followed river valleys, including the Taku, Stikine, and Alsek. These routes crossed mountain passes, notably Chilkat and Chilcoot, near present-day Haines, Alaska. Like many special activities, trading had religious significance. Traders prepared themselves by fasting, consulting a shaman, and then hosting a feast. Before departing on an expedition, they painted their faces to appear attractive to their trading partners. Goods were hauled up river by canoe, then carried by slaves in large baskets fitted with shoulder and forehead straps. Each backpack of a male slave held one hundred or more pounds while each woman carried about sixty-five pounds. Dogs labored with saddle bags weighing up to twenty-five pounds. A good trader always brought along an elderly woman who shrewdly bargained for the best deals.

Among the Tlingit's most valued imports were walrus ivory from the Inuit who lived near the Bering Sea, canoes from the Haida, and dentalia shells from other native peoples in the south. Through trade,

The Tlingit traded clams, mussels, and other sea creatures that they gathered along the edge of the water.

These women displayed their handicrafts, including these baskets woven from strips of cedar.

they also acquired slaves, furs, and skin garments in exchange for Chilkat blankets, seaweed, fish oil, and many other products. They traded for moose and caribou hides, leather thongs and sinews, and copper ore. They exchanged cedar baskets, fish oil, shells, and smoked seafood for finely-sewn moccasins, birch wood bows wrapped with porcupine gut, and snowshoes. The Tlingit traded dentalia shells from Vancouver Island for rare items of copper and wood from the Inuit of Siberia and Alaska.

The Tlingit also regularly traded among themselves. Those living on the islands traded with mainland villages for dressed hides, rabbit and marmot skin blankets, moose hide shirts, and skin trousers with moccasins attached. They sought cranberries preserved in oil, strawberry cakes, candlefish oil, horn spoons, woven blankets, and spruce root baskets. In exchange, the islanders offered sea otter pelts, dried venison, seal oil, dried seaweed, clams, mussels, and other sea creatures, along with dried fish, especially halibut, salmon, and herring.

When European traders arrived, many Tlingit became wealthy during the era of the fur trade. All the native peoples living in the interior longed for manufactured goods, including guns, gunpowder, shot, steel traps, knives, hatchets, and needles and thread, along with cloth and blankets. They also wanted staples such as flour, rice, and beans, as well as tobacco and molasses. During this time, the Tlingit were fairly effective in monopolizing trade in the region. They once journeyed as far as three hundred miles to destroy a post of the Hudson's Bay Company.

4. Beliefs

The Tlingit undertook
many rituals to assure
good fortune in hunting
and fishing.

THE TLINGIT REVERED ANIMALS AND OBJECTS IN NATURE. THEY BELIEVED they had souls like those of people. They respected animals that could bring misfortune or help, especially animals that gave their lives to sustain the families of hunters and fishermen. Before they hunted or fished, men purified themselves and as they pursued game, they undertook special rituals. When they came home after an expedition, they offered thanks to the animals that had generously allowed themselves to be killed.

Every house and clan sought the protection of a shaman. Most were men, but women occasionally became shamans. It was believed that these powerful shamans possessed remarkable abilities to heal the body and the spirit. They not only effected cures, but also influenced the weather, brought good fortune in hunting, foretold the future, exposed witches, and spoke with the dead. A shaman could be effective only if he were consulted in time and if another shaman was not working against him.

A shaman acquired his powers from the spirits he called upon in a sacred song. To remain pure and keep their powers strong, shamans often fasted and went without water. Neither a shaman nor his wife ever cut their hair. At the approach of his own death, a shaman sought out a younger relative to take his place. The young person became dizzy and ill until he or she accepted this obligation. The Tlingit held shamans in high regard. Yet, at one time, officers of the U.S. Navy punished shamans by shaving their heads.

The Tlingit relied on shamans, such as this old man, to heal their injuries and illnesses and to ensure spiritual well-being.

Potlatches

Native peoples of the Northwest, including the Tlingit, often came together for important celebrations known as potlatches. The term *potlatch* comes from the Nootka word *patshatl*, which means "giving" or "gift." In these feasts, nobles generously shared their wealth by feeding their guests and lavishing gifts on them. By accepting the food and gifts, the guests acknowledged the wealth and rank of the host. During the potlatch, the host family displayed their clan crests through songs and dances. Crests also adorned masks and other finely-crafted objects—even the serving dishes. Afterwards, the guests hosted their own potlatches to share what they had with their hosts and establish claims to property and rights to names.

All the coastal tribes of the Northwest held potlatches to mark key moments in the cycle of life. For example, the Tsimshian held a potlatch to mark the death of a leader, and the Haida celebrated the dedication of a chief's house and later his death with a potlatch. The Tlingit held potlatches at three vital occasions—piercing the ears of noble children, funerals, and memorials when an heir assumed the position of leadership left by his mother's brother (uncle). During winter, houses also hosted potlatches to bring together spirits, ancestors, and the living to celebrate changes in rank and lives of family members. Partitions inside the house were removed to make a large room for guests who came from near and far. At these potlatches, guests respectfully called upon the spirits for help in feeding, clothing, and healing people.

*G*uests dressed in ceremonial garments, including hats and ornate jewelry,
attend a Tlingit potlatch.

The arrival of Europeans brought many devastating changes to the native peoples of the Northwest that affected the tradition of potlatches. Hundreds of people, including many nobles, perished in terrible epidemics of measles and smallpox for which the native people had little or no resistance. Commoners then claimed the titles, rights, and wealth of the deceased nobles. Beginning in the 1830s, the Hudson's Bay Company offered valuable goods in exchange for furs, and a hardworking commoner could amass enough wealth to host a potlatch and lay claim to a high name. These commoners tended to use their newly acquired riches more as bribes than as gifts. People of different tribes also gathered in villages around forts and trading posts. This close everyday contact with new neighbors led to a cycle of extravagant, rival potlatches to establish the social positions of house, clan, and tribal chiefs among the Tlingit and other coastal people.

The potlatch came to be viewed as an elaborate game and a foolish extravagance corrupted by trade goods. Officials, missionaries, and native converts in both the United States and Canada opposed the potlatch. They did not understand how people could devote years of their lives to amassing wealth only to give everything away. Potlatches were outlawed in both countries and only recently have the Tlingit been allowed to host these complex events that hold such deep meaning to them.

Storytelling

According to Tlingit beliefs, humans and animals are closely related. The animals who were once people fled into the forest and sea when Raven brought light to the world. They believe that animals may assume human form, as in one story in which a bear marries a woman. People, such as Salmon Boy, can also become animals. Of all the animals, it is thought that Bear and Raven are most like people. Walking on his hind legs, Bear hunts for the same foods as do people. With hand-like paws, he catches salmon and picks berries and nuts. Raven, moving cleverly between the human and the animal worlds, both generously helps people and plays tricks on them. He is also imbued with human flaws of selfishness and greed. These relationships between people and animals often emphasize the survival of the Tlingit, especially the vital task of acquiring food.

Here is one such story about how a Tlingit man and later his wife and children provided for others:

Man and Monster

Somewhere in the north, a young man from a noble family married a high-ranking young woman from a neighboring village. His mother-in-law lived with the newlyweds and she disliked the youth. He seemed only interested in gambling and often stayed out very late at night. So, after every meal in the evening, the mother-in-law told the slaves, "Let the fire go out." She did not want her son-in-law to enjoy a warm meal when he finally stumbled home. When he at last arrived, late at night, the mother-in-law whispered mockingly to her daughter, "I suppose he has been hard at work, felling a tree for me." Early the next morning the young man again left the clan house and did not return until well after dark. This happened every day, and his wife was dismayed. But she thought it was useless to say anything to him.

That summer all the people of the village, including the youthful gambler, journeyed to the river to fish for salmon. He did help in catching and drying the salmon, but afterwards he went into the woods and built a house beside a lake. With a stone ax, he then felled a large tree into the lake. He made wedges of hardwood with which to partially split the log, wedging a crossbeam in between to keep the two halves apart. He was making a trap because he had heard that a monster lived in the deep waters of that lake.

Baiting a hook and line with salmon, he waited for quite a while. When the line at last jiggled, he pulled rapidly. Caught on the hook, the monster rose to the surface between the two halves of the log. The young man then yanked the crossbeam so that the halves of the log sprang together and caught the monster's head.

The monster soon died and the young man dragged its body from the water. It had strong copperlike teeth and claws. The young man carefully skinned the monster with the claws and teeth attached to the shaggy hide. After the hide had properly cured, he crawled inside and slipped into the water. The hide swam away with him, carrying him to the monster's beautiful home under the lake. After he came up, the man hid the skin in a hole in a tree and went home, saying not a word about his adventure.

As winter approached, everyone went back to the village. For a while they had food, but the following spring there was a famine.

One morning the man told his wife, "I am going away. If you hear a raven before I return do not look for me anymore."

He retrieved the monster's skin and went to the beach not far from the village. Plunging into the water, he discovered that he could swim in the sea. He caught a king salmon. He carried the fish to the village and left it on the beach near the house where he lived with his wife and mother-in-law.

The next morning his mother-in-law arose early, walked outside, and found the salmon. She believed it had washed ashore. "I have found a fine big salmon!" she proudly announced. Her family cooked the salmon and shared its meat with everyone in the village, as was the custom of their people. The next evening the young man caught two salmon and left them on the beach, where his mother-in-law found them. When he went to bed the young man told his wife that he was getting those salmon, but not to say a word to anyone.

The third time that he brought salmon and his mother-in-law discovered them, she began to deeply ponder the situation. Her son-in-law now slept all day and she chastised him, "If I did not pick up salmon, the whole village would be starving."

Afterwards, he and his wife laughed about her comments.

The next evening he plunged into the sea and caught a very large halibut that he placed in front of his mother-in-law's house. When she found the fish, the mother-in-law was very pleased with herself. She now thought, "A spirit must be bringing luck to me."

The young man next caught a seal that he laid near the woman's house. He said nothing to his mother-in-law, although she belittled him more than ever. When a canoe landed at the village, she sneered, "I suppose my son-in-law has brought a load of seal."

That night the mother-in-law pretended that a spirit visited and said to her, "I am the spirit that finds all this food for you." As she lay in bed, she told her husband, "Have a mask made for me, and let them name it Food Finding Spirit."

So, the next day her husband sent for the best carver in the village and had the mask made for her. He also had an apron made, fringed with puffin beaks and other fine ornaments. Wearing the mask, the mother-in-law walked around the village, shaking a rattle, and everyone believed that she was a powerful shaman. She talked often of her spirits and the nobles spoke highly of her. However, she gave little food to her son-in-law and derided him more than ever, "Leave only a few scraps for Sleeping Man."

The young man kept saying to his wife, "Always listen for the ravens. If you hear a raven before I come you will know that something has happened to me." The young woman worried about her husband and she was sad that her mother treated him so badly. The next day the young man left a sea lion at the mother-in-law's house and she was very proud. She invited all the people to a feast and boasted, "It has been this way from olden times. The chiefs of a village are always lucky."

Although she actually had not a single spirit, the mother-in-law believed that she was a great noble of her people. When the young man left a whale for her, she was especially haughty. She filled boxes with oil and all kinds of food that she sold to the people. But she shared very little with her daughter and son-in-law.

One night, the young man said to his wife, "If you find that I am dead in the skin, do not take me out of it. Put me and the skin in the place where I hid it, and you will get help."

This went on for a long time. The young man decided not to catch another whale, because he had had such a hard time with the first one. He continued to bring food to his mother-in-law who persisted in treating him spitefully. One day he came upon two whales. He caught and tried to swim ashore with both of them. He worked all night, but just as he neared the beach, the raven called and he died at the edge of the water.

When his wife heard the cry of the raven, she quickly dressed, but she did not go outside. Then her mother walked out and found the two whales washed ashore with the monster lying between them. Everyone went down to the beach and when they saw the monster with fins on his back, long ears, and a very long tail, they cried, "That terrible monster must be the old woman's spirit."

Weeping loudly, the young woman then came down to the beach. She cried out to her lost husband.

The young woman turned on her mother and demanded, "Where is your spirit now? You are a storyteller. You have no spirit. That is why my husband died."

Everyone thought there was something wrong with her. They asked themselves, "What does that noble woman mean by saying that the monster is her husband?"

The young woman told her mother, "Is this your Food Finding Spirit? If so, how is it that your spirit died? Spirits never die. If this is your spirit, bring it to life again."

Then, as the young woman approached the monster, she said, "Some of you who are good and pure, come and help me."

As the people came near, they saw that the young woman's husband had died as he struggled to open the jaws of the monster— at the very moment that the raven had cried. They helped to place the body of the young man and the monster's skin in the hollow of a tree.

Thereafter, the old woman was so ashamed of herself that she would not set foot outside her house. She soon withered away and died.

Every evening, the young woman went to the foot of the tree and grieved tearfully for her lost husband. However, one night she noticed a ripple on the water and saw the monster in the lake. In the voice of her husband the monster called to her, "Come here, my beloved. Climb onto my back and hold tight." She did so, and together they swam down to the monster's beautiful home deep beneath the waters of the lake, where they live to this day. This monster and his wife now bring good fortune to anyone who sees them—as do the daughters who were born to them. These children are the Daughters of the Creek who live at the headwaters of every stream.

*L*ate in the afternoon, the sun reflects off the clouds and water in the land where the Tlingit have lived for many generations.

5. Changing World

Keeping warm
in the cold, damp air,
Tlingit women traded
with other native people
and later with the
Russians and Americans.

TLINGIT LIFE STARTED TO CHANGE AS SOON AS EUROPEANS BEGAN TO VISIT the coast of Alaska. In 1741, Russian explorer Alexsey Chirikov became the first European to touch upon the shores of southeastern Alaska. In 1775, Spaniard Bruno de Hezeta ventured into the region. He was followed by Frenchman Jean François de Galaup, Comte de La Pérouse in 1786, Italian Alejandro Malaspina in 1791, and Englishman George Vancouver in 1793. However, the Russians were the first to actually establish a settlement along the waters. In 1799, they constructed a military fort at Sitka. Three years later, Tlingit warriors under the leadership of Katlian (also spelled Katlyan) attacked and destroyed the post. However, in 1804, the Russians rebuilt the fort, which became the headquarters of the Russian-American Fur Company from 1808 to 1867. During this time, the Tlingit traded with the Russians for metal tools, cloth, and other goods, but otherwise tried to continue their ancestral way of life. Between 1835 and 1839, however, many people died in outbreaks of smallpox and other diseases. As they recovered from these sweeping epidemics, some Tlingit people converted to the Russian Orthodox religion.

Operating out of Canada, the Hudson's Bay Company acquired rights to trade in southeastern Alaska from the Russian-American Fur Company. Soon, goods manufactured in Europe began to pour into the region. Native people, including the Tlingit, eagerly sought these trade items, which included steel chisels and axes for carving totem poles and other wooden objects. Dealing with both the Russian American Company and the Hudson's Bay Company, the Tlingit developed an extensive trade network in which they controlled much

The Tlingit eagerly sought expensive trade items, such as this ornate chest, from the Russians.

of the trade among the tribes living in the interior of Alaska. By the 1850s, they were trading as far south as Puget Sound in the present-day state of Washington, where they bartered with Americans for firearms and whiskey.

The Russians maintained a strong presence in Alaska until 1867. However, the great empire was staggering from its losses in the Crimean War and internal turmoil. In desperate need of funds, the tsar agreed to sell Alaska to the United States for $7.2 million. At the time, many people in the United States objected to the deal, which they mockingly referred to as "Seward's Folly," after Secretary of State William H. Seward who encouraged the purchase. The Tlingit bitterly opposed this sale as well. In their view, Alaska did not belong to Russia and it had no right to sell the land to another country. They argued that

This Russian church, as it appeared in 1889, towered over the village of Sitka on the coast of southeastern Alaska.

if anyone owned Alaska, it was the Tlingit and the other native peoples who lived there. The Tlingit protested the purchase and refused to submit to the United States. To assert authority over the Tlingit, the U.S. Navy shelled the villages of Kake and Wrangell in 1869 and destroyed Angoon in 1882.

Through the remainder of the nineteenth century, waves of American soldiers, miners, and settlers came north to seek their fortune in gold mines, fishing, and other enterprises. They mistreated the Tlingit and other Alaskan natives. Although they had lived there for thousands of years, Alaskan natives were treated as inferior to the newcomers. They were allowed few or no rights. Although the Tlingit held aboriginal title to the territory, they were not permitted to file land claims in a gold rush near Juneau in 1880. When commercial fishing and canning operations were established in the 1870s and 1880s, the Tlingit received lower wages than other workers—if they could get a job at all. In 1897–1898, the Klondike gold rush brought more jobs and money to the region, but Alaska natives benefitted little.

In the latter years of the nineteenth century, the Tlingit also came to be dominated by missionaries from the United States and Canada, especially Presbyterians, who established churches in their midst. Most coastal Tlingit had long since converted to the Russian Orthodox faith after the smallpox epidemic that raged from 1835 to 1839. However, Presbyterian missionaries now criticized them for using the Russian alphabet and expressing the beliefs of the Russian Orthodox religion. Many other Protestant and Catholic missionaries

By 1900, many Tlingit people had abandoned their villages and moved into cities where they worked in canneries.

also descended upon the Tlingit. Competing for the souls of the Tlingit, these missionaries tried to impose their own version of Christianity on the native people and to extinguish all ancestral beliefs and customs. The bawdy cry of Raven was silenced, as traditional stories gave way to those of a great flood or other stories drawn from the Bible.

By the turn of the century, many Tlingit had also abandoned a way of life based on hunting, fishing, and gathering. Many villages were completely deserted as people moved to cities to seek jobs in canneries. Some went as far as British Columbia looking for work. Many journeyed even farther away to the sprawling fields of eastern Washington where they picked hops. The Tlingit held few, if any, potlatches, which were no longer considered significant to families and communities. The dances, rituals, and art objects related to these great celebrations were nearly forgotten. The Tlingit sold many of their cherished objects to museums and collectors—or the priceless ancestral objects were stolen. However, a few villages resisted these overwhelming changes and struggled desperately to continue the ways of their ancestors.

Tlingit Language

As the Tlingit spread northward, their language came to vary somewhat from one region to the next. As noted by the well-known authority on Tlingit culture, Frederica de Laguna, "There are slight differences in pronunciation between the quick-speaking southerners and the more drawling, louder northerners." And among the northerners, especially along the Gulf coast, the sounds are pronounced farther back in the throat.

Here are some examples of the Tlingit language based on the *English-Tlingit Dictionary*, compiled by Constance Naish and Gillian Story. Some letters are pronounced as in English, but Tlingit is a very complex language with eight vowels and forty-three consonants. The following examples have been simplified, but offer an idea of how to pronounce a number of Tlingit words.

The vowels are generally pronounced as follows:

a	as in w*a*s
e	as in t*e*n
i	as in h*i*t
u	as in p*u*sh
aa	as in f*a*ther
ei	as in v*ei*n
ee	as in s*ee*k
oo	as in m*oo*n

The consonants have many variations with no equivalents in English and their diacritic marks have been omitted in this brief vocabulary. Note, however, that the Tlingit *x* is pronounced something like *sh* but farther back in the mouth, like the *ch* in the German word *ach*. Fourteen Tlingit sounds are made with an accompanying glottal stop, or catch-in-the-breath sound. These are represented by an apostrophe (') after the letter.

People

aunt (father's sister)	at
aunt (mother's sister)	tlak'w
brother, older	honxw
brother, younger	keek
child	ut k'utsk'oo
daughter	see
father	eesh
grandchild	duchxun
grandparent	leelk'w
husband	xox
mother	tlah
sister, older	shutx
sister, younger	keek
son	yeet
uncle (father's brother)	sunee
uncle (mother's brother)	kak
wife	shut

Parts of the Body

arm	jigei
ear	gok
eye	wak
foot, leg	x'oos
hand	jin
head	shuh
heart	teix'

mouth	x'eh
neck	lidex'
nose	loh
skin	dook

Natural World

bay	geey
beach	eek
cliff	gil'
forest	as gootoo
glacier	sit'
ice	t'eex'
iceberg	xatl
island	x'at'
land, earth	tl'utk
mainland	tleiyun
mountain	shah
ocean	eil'
river	heen
sun	gagaan
valley	shanux
waterfall	x'as

Sky and Weather

fog	kogwas'
frost	kuxwan

moon	dis
Northern Lights	gees'ook
rain	seew, soow
seasons:	
spring	takw eetee
summer	kotan
fall	yeis
winter	takw
sky, cloudy	goos'
sky, clear	xats'
snow, wet	kuxluheen, kukluheen
snow, dry	dleit kuketsk
star	kotx uyunuhah
sun	gugan

Mammals

bear, black	s'eek
bear, brown	xoots
caribou	wutsix
dog	keitl
moose	dzisk'w
otter, land	kooshdah
rabbit	gux
sheep, mountain	junwoo
squirrel	kunuls'ak
wolf	gooch

6. The Tlingit Today

Many Tlingit, such as these young people of Saxman Village, keep their traditions alive through dances in the clan house.

In 1740, there were at least ten thousand Tlingit living in what is now southeastern Alaska and Canada. Despite widespread epidemics and other hardships, by the 1990s, there were about 14,000 Tlingit in the United States and 1,200 in Canada. Many people continue to live in ancestral villages, but others now make their home in Ketchikan, Juneau, and other cities in the Northwest. Major Tlingit villages include Yakutat, Hoonah, Klukwan, Angoon, Kake, Craig, and Klawock.

In 1912, the Alaska Native Brotherhood (ANB) was founded by Presbyterian natives who sought rapid assimilation along with economic opportunities, land rights, and an end to discrimination to their people. Soon after, the Alaska Native Sisterhood (ANS) was established with similar goals. (However, in the late 1960s, both organizations reversed their positions and came to favor the preser-

Members of the Alaska Native Brotherhood, an organization that has played a major role in preserving Tlingit culture, pose for this 1930 photograph.

vation of Tlingit language and customs.) In 1924, native peoples were allowed to vote in Alaska. But most natives, including the Tlingit, were still considered members of a lower social and economic class. They remained segregated from other Alaskans. Despite repeated efforts by the Tlingit, schools in Alaska were not integrated until 1949.

After the Indian Reorganization Act was extended by Congress in 1936 to include Alaska, a few villages incorporated and supported themselves through small industries. Following World War II, the Tlingit also sought to reclaim a portion of their land. Joining with the Haida, who have communities at the southern tip of the Alaskan panhandle, they established the Central Council of Tlingit and Haida which in 1968 settled a land claim for $7.5 million. According to the preamble of the council's constitution, its purpose is to "preserve their identity as Indian tribes and the identity and culture of their members and their descendants as Indian people [and to] provide for the exercise of their tribal sovereignty." Today, the Tlingit-Haida Central Council is the federally recognized tribal organization of the Tlingit in Alaska. The council is made up of delegates elected from fourteen communities in southeastern Alaska and other communities.

In 1971, according to terms of the Alaska Native Claims Settlement Act, twelve regional corporations, including Sealaska, which encompasses Tlingit territory, and about two hundred village corporations were established. The Tlingit and other native peoples of Alaska also received nearly $1 billion and title to forty-four million acres in exchange for giving up ancestral claims to all other lands. In the early 1970s, the Sealaska Corporation received 280,000 acres of timberland and $200 million. Each village received surface land rights while the corporation was granted subsurface rights. These corporations are now involved in logging, fishing, and development of the land. These initiatives are leading to an economic resurgence among the Tlingit and other Native Alaskans.

No more than four hundred Tlingit ever lived inland. The Inland Tlingit came into greater contact with outsiders in the 1940s when the Alaska Highway opened. In the 1960s radio and television brought more rapid changes. Today, most young people on the coast and interior speak only English. The Teslin (Yukon) and the Taku River (British Columbia) Tlingit are recognized by the government of Canada. The Teslin Tlingit are now part of the Carcross Tagish First Nation. The Teslin Tlingit Council Band, as part of the Daxa Nation, has three reserves in the southwest of Teslin in Canada. In the early 1990s, the population totaled 482 people living in 119 households. Since the late 1940s the Department of Indian Affairs has required elections for leadership positions. Clan leaders include a chief and five counselors. Tlingit children attend schools managed by the band or the province. There are other facilities on the reserves including administration buildings and a longhouse, clinic, and recreation center.

Despite their often remote locations, most Tlingit villages now have electric service and satellite television. Every village has an elementary school and at least one church. A few also have a high school. Most children, however, have to travel to a larger city to

*T*lingit children attend native schools or travel long distances to attend public schools in Haines, Alaska, and other communities.

attend high school. People still follow the clan system, although its influence has faded in recent years. Now Christian, most Tlingit people, especially those living in cities, have abandoned traditional ways. Very few people can speak Tlingit, although the language is now being taught in the schools. The ANB and ANS are also working to renew the traditional culture of the Tlingit. Important ceremonies, notably potlatching, singing, dancing, and crest arts, have also enjoyed a revival in recent years. A vigorous political, economic, and cultural revival is now underway, and the Tlingit are determined that their children will have a brighter future.

More about

the Tlingit

Time Line

1741 Russian explorers enter the coastal waters of the Tlingit and other Alaskan natives.

1786 First confirmed encounter of the Tlingit with Europeans when Jean François de Galaup, Comte de La Pérouse, a French explorer, enters Lituya Bay and stays in Alaska for three months.

1808–1867 Russians establish trading settlements along the coast of Alaska.

1835–1839 Epidemics of smallpox and other diseases sweep through Tlingit communities.

1867 At the initiative of William H. Seward, the United States purchases Alaska from Russia for $7,200,000.

1884 The Organic Act is passed by Congress, allowing for a basic form of government in Alaska.

1887 The General Allotment Act, also known as the Dawes Act, divides reservation lands into small tracts that are allocated to individual tribal members. The remaining land is sold by the government.

1897 The Act of June 6th, 1897 prohibits the use of native subsistence fish traps in Alaska. The Klondike gold rush begins on July 6. In less than two months 30,000 men pour into the territory.

1900 Congress enacts the Carter Code, which extends the civil laws of Oregon Territory to Alaska.

1902 President Theodore Roosevelt establishes the Tongass National Forest. Eventually, protected lands include nearly sixteen million acres in southeast Alaska.

1906 The Native Allotment Act grants 160 acres of public land to adult native peoples. Few tracts were awarded, however, because the Bureau of Land Management would not recognize subsistence use of the land for hunting and fishing as proof of "use and occupancy."

1912 Alaska becomes a territory with a two-house legislature. The Alaska Native Brotherhood holds its first organizational meeting. Peter Simpson is elected as the first president of the organization.

1922 Voting rights of Alaska natives are affirmed when W. L. Paul Sr. successfully defends Charlie Jones who is charged with illegal voting.

1924 Alaskan natives become U.S. citizens. The Alexander Fish Bill outlaws subsistence fishing in southeast Alaska.

1926 W. L. Paul Sr. is the first Alaska native elected to the territorial house of representatives.

1929 In court proceedings, W. L. Paul Sr. establishes the right of native children to attend public schools. An ANB convention at Haines resolves to pursue the Tlingit and Haida land claims.

1934 The Indian Reorganization Act allows greater independence for native peoples, but Alaska is excluded in the law.

1935 The Jurisdictional Act creates a governing body for the Tlingit and Haida.

1936 At the request of the ANB, the Indian Reorganization Act is amended to include Alaska.

1939 The ANB organizes the Central Council and elects Andrew Hope as president. However, the U.S. Department of the Interior challenges the legitimacy of the organization and another election is held at the 1941 convention.

1945 After many years of effort by ANB, the territorial legislature passes the Anti-Discrimination Act.

1946 Mt. Edgecumbe High School opens in Sitka, a small community in southeast Alaska. Many future native leaders attend this native boarding school. Frank Peratrovich, an Alaska native, is elected president of the Alaska senate.

1949 Alaska schools are integrated.

1959 On January 3, Alaska becomes the forty-ninth state. One of the first laws passed by the new Alaska state legislature outlaws the use of fish traps.

1965 The Central Council amends the Jurisdictional Act of 1935, thereby recognizing the council as the governing body of the Tlingit and Haida, and reducing the authority of the Bureau of Indian Affairs (BIA).

1966 On October 18, the first meeting of the Alaska Federation of Natives is held in Anchorage.

1968 The U.S. Court of Claims awards the Tlingit and the Haida people $7.5 million for lands taken to form the Tongass National Forest and Glacier Bay National Monument. Funds are not actually awarded to the Central Council until 1970.

1971 On December 18, the Alaska Native Claims Settlement Act takes effect.

1972 The Indian Education Act is passed.

1978 The Indian Child Welfare Act is passed by Congress.

1982 For the first time, the Tlingit, Haida, and Tsimshian nations come together in a celebration of their native cultures.

1984 The Andrew Hope Building is completed and becomes the headquarters of the Central Council.

1993 The Central Council is removed from the list of federally recognized tribes.

1994 U.S. Congress restores the Central Council to the list of federally recognized tribes.

Notable People

William G. Demmert Jr. (1934–), university professor and administrator, was born in Klawock, Alaska. He graduated from Seattle Pacific College and then taught at Forks, Washington, from 1960 to 1964. In 1965, he moved to Fairbanks where he lived until moving back to his hometown in 1968. There, he was chief administrator of the public school system until 1970. Meanwhile, in 1969, Demmert, who is of Tlingit and Dakota Sioux descent, was invited to attend the First Convocation of American Indian Scholars. As a result of this meeting, Demmert helped to found the National Indian Educational Association, and became one of the original directors.

William G. Demmert Jr.

While attending Harvard University from 1970 to 1973, he worked for the passage of the Indian Education Act of 1972. He also joined the U.S. Department of Education as an official in Indian education in 1972 and received his doctorate from Harvard the following year. He has since published many articles in the field of education.

He has taught at many prominent universities, including the University of Alaska, Stanford University, the University of Washington, and Harvard University. He also held positions in several federal agencies and programs, such as the Indian Nations at Risk Force, dedicated to improving the quality of education for Native American children.

Katlian (Katlyan) (active early 1800s), a Tlingit leader, who was born and raised in the coastal village of Sitka, led the Tlingit in several conflicts against Russian traders and colonists in southeastern Alaska. The Russians arrived on the Aleutian Islands after Vitus Bering undertook an exploratory voyage in 1741 and confirmed that Alaska was a body of land separate from Asia. The Russians forced the Aleuts to help catch sea otters whose fur was highly prized. Gradually moving eastward, the Russians established a fort near Sitka in 1799. Three years later, Katlian led an attack on the fort and drove the Russians from Sitka. Katlian and his men held the fort for two years until a force of about 120 Russians and 1,000 Aleuts returned with cannons. They bombarded the fort and the soldiers attacked. Katlian and his men retreated, but they remained hostile to the Russians. In 1805, Katlian attacked a post at Yakutat. The traders appealed to the Russian navy for protection and in 1818 a Russian warship began to patrol Sitka Harbor. However, Katlian and other Tlingit warriors continued their hostilities, which became one of the reasons the Russians decided to sell Alaska to the United States in 1867.

Elizabeth W. Peratrovich (Kaaxgal-aat) (1911–1958), a prominent civil rights leader, was born in Petersburg, Alaska, where she attended elementary school. She went to high school in Ketchikan and then attended Western College of Education in Bellingham, Washington. In 1931, she married Roy Peratrovich. Ten years later, they moved back to Alaska with their family. Elizabeth and her husband became active in the Alaska Native Brotherhood and Alaska Native Sisterhood, organizations that sought to gain civil rights for native peoples. When the Peratroviches moved to Juneau, Elizabeth was grand camp (chapter) president of the ANS and Roy was grand-president of the regional ANB.

The organizations had already helped Alaska natives gain the right to vote in 1922. Yet native children were not allowed to attend public schools in Juneau and the ANB sued to integrate the school district. At that time, the Peratroviches also encountered signs that read "No Natives Allowed" and "No Dogs or Indians Allowed." They were outraged when they were not allowed to purchase a home in a neighborhood they liked. The Peratroviches confronted the Alaskan territorial legislature with these issues of discrimination. They lobbied daily until an antidiscrimination bill was proposed. Elizabeth offered vivid testimony that swayed the legislature to vote 11–5 in favor of the bill outlawing discrimination in housing, public accommodations, and restaurants in Alaska.

Elizabeth W. Peratrovich

On February 16, 1945, the act was signed into law. It was the first antidiscrimination law in the United States. While Alaska was still a territory, it made significant advances in civil rights in large part because of the efforts of Elizabeth and Roy Peratrovich. In 1988, February 16 was officially declared Elizabeth W. Peratrovich Day in Alaska. Elizabeth died of cancer at the age of forty-seven, yet she is remembered every year on this date.

Shakes (Shaikes) (active 1800s) was the hereditary name of an important family and several Tlingit chiefs who lived on Wrangell Island in what is now known as the Alexander Archipelago of southeastern Alaska. The name Shakes was first noted by the 1841–1842 expedition of Sir George Simpson. The Shakes became one of the wealthiest and most powerful families because of the fur trade on their island and up the Stikine River on the Alaska mainland. They traded with the Russians and the English. After the United States purchased Alaska in 1867, missionaries came to Wrangell Island, but Chief Shakes rejected all their efforts to convert him. Shakes received assurances of financial assistance from the United States for schools and economic development, but the promises were never fulfilled. In the early 1900s, the last chief of the Shakes lineage established a museum with an impressive collection of art objects of native peoples of the Northwest coast. The last Chief Shakes died in 1944.

Rosita Worl (Yeidiklatsokw), (1937–   ), anthropologist, activist, and educator, was born in Petersburg, Alaska, and raised in Haines, Juneau, and Petersburg. Her traditional home village is Klukwan on the Chilkat River, not far from Haines. She attended a mission boarding school in Haines for three years, then after returning home she learned Tlingit traditions from her mother and grandparents. Worl also learned a great deal from her mother's dedicated activities as a union organizer in canneries. After graduating from Juneau High School, Worl attended Alaska Methodist University where she graduated magna cum laude in 1972. She earned a master's degree in social anthropology from Harvard University in 1975. She received a Ford Foundation fellowship to pursue her studies, including postgraduate work, from 1972 to 1975. She has since been a research anthropologist and co-curator of the "Tlingit Clans and Corporations" exhibition at the National Museum of Natural History. She has also worked on several state projects in Alaska on behalf of native peoples.

As an anthropologist, Worl has worked in the field on many arduous projects in Alaska and Canada. Her work with the Inuit of the far north helped to preserve their right to hunt whales. She also undertook research on the impact of oil development on the native peoples of Alaska. She then moved to Anchorage, where she worked as an assistant professor of anthropology at the University of Alaska. As a member of the Alaska Native Brotherhood and the Alaska Native Sisterhood, Worl has worked for the social welfare and civil rights of Alaska natives. She has been one of the individuals responsible for the cultural renaissance of the Tlingit. She has served on the boards of the Klukwan Heritage Foundation, the Alaska State Arts Council, Traditional Native Arts Panel, and the Folk Arts Panel of the National Endowment for the Arts.

Rosita Worl

Worl has received several awards for her work, including the Alaska Press Club Award for Excellence for Return of Native Artifacts, 1987–88. She is also active in Keepers of the Treasures, Cultural Council of American Indians, Alaska Natives and Native Hawaiians, and she has served as vice-chair of the Sealaska Heritage Foundation. Her research and writing emphasize the traditions of the Tlingit. Among her essays is "History of Southeastern Alaska Since 1867," published in the *Handbook of North American Indians, Northwest Coast*, Volume 7, by the Smithsonian Institution Press. When asked how she maintains such a daunting schedule, Worl responded, "I require very little sleep."

Glossary

clan Group of lineages, or families, descended from common ancestors.

clan house Large dwelling in which several related families from the same clan live together.

commoner One of the classes of people in Tlingit society who did not own houses or other valuable property.

crest figure A bird, fish, or other animal that symbolizes one's lineage, often painted or carved on houses, totem poles, and other personal property.

dugout A boat made by hollowing out a large log.

kwan Groups of people living in the same geographic area.

lineage A family line, a group of people descended from a common ancestor.

matrilineal Tracing descent through the mother's side of the family.

moieties The two halves of society; the Tlingit moieties are Raven and Wolf (sometimes called Eagle in the north).

noble Highest social class of the Tlingit.

potlatch Lavish ceremonial feast held on special occasions in which the host gives away many valuable presents.

reserve In Canada, name for an Indian reservation.

Raven Large black bird of the crow family revered by the Tlingit.

roe A mass of fish eggs.

smokehouse Building in which fish or meat is preserved by smoking and drying.

spawn Laying and fertilizing a large number of eggs, said of fish.

Tlingit canoe Canoe, or dugout, made of red cedar with a high prow, often emblazoned with the crest of its owner.

totem pole Poles carved from red cedar on which people displayed their crests and related family histories.

Further Information

There are many excellent materials available for learning more about the Tlingit. The following books and Web sites were consulted while researching and writing this book. The two stories in *The Tlingit* were adapted from stories compiled by John Reed Swanton and published in *Tlingit Myths and Texts*.

Anatolii, Bishop of Tomsk. *Tlingit Indians of Alaska*. Fairbanks: University of Alaska Press, 1985.

Beck, Mary Giraudo. *Heroes & Heroines: Tlingit-Haida Legend*. Anchorage, AK: Northwest Books, 1989.

Cruikshank, Julie. *Life Lived Like a Story: Life Stories of Three Yukon Native Elders*. Lincoln: University of Nebraska Press, 1990.

Dauenhauer, Nora Marks and Richard Dauenhauer. *Haa Shuka, Our Ancestors. Tlingit Oral Narratives*. Seattle: University of Washington Press; Juneau: Sealaska Heritage Foundation, 1987.

Dauenhauer, Nora. *Life Woven with Song*. Tucson: University of Arizona Press, 2000.

De Laguna, Frederica. "Tlingit," in *Handbook of North American Indians*, vol. 7, pp. 204–228. Washington: Smithsonian Institution, 1990.

De Laguna, Frederica. *Under Mount Saint Elias: the History and Culture of the Yakutat Tlingit*. Washington: Smithsonian Institution Press, 1972.

Emmons, George Thornton. *The Tlingit Indians*. Seattle: University of Washington Press; New York: American Museum of Natural History, 1991.

Encyclopedia of North American Indians. Tarrytown, NY: Marshall Cavendish, 1997.

Goldschmidt, Walter R., and Theodore H. Haas. *Haa Aani—Our Land. Tlingit and Haida Land Rights and Use*. Seattle: University of Washington Press; Juneau: Sealaska Heritage Foundation, 1998.

Johansen, Bruce E., and Donald A. Grinde Jr. *The Encyclopedia of Native American Biography*. New York: Henry Holt, 1997.

Jonaitis, Aldona. *Art of the Northern Tlingit*. Seattle: University of Washington Press, 1986.

Kan, Sergei. *Symbolic Immortality: The Tlingit Potlatch of the Nineteenth Century*. Washington: Smithsonian Institution Press, 1989.

Kan, Sergei. *Memory Eternal: Tlingit Culture and Russian Orthodox Christianity Through Two Centuries*. Seattle: University of Washington Press, 1999.

Kaiper, Dan and Nan. *Tlingit: Their Art, Culture & Legends*. Saanichton, BC; Seattle: Hancock House, 1978.

Krause, Aurel. *The Tlingit Indians: Results of a Trip to the Northwest Coast of America and the Bering Straits*. Seattle: University of Washington Press, 1956.

Malinowski, Sharon, and Sheets, Anna. *The Gale Encyclopedia of Native American Tribes*. Detroit: Gale Research, 1998.

Malinowski, Sharon. *Notable Native Americans*. Detroit: Gale Research, 1995.

Miller, Jay. *Tsimshian Culture: A Light through the Ages*. Lincoln: University of Nebraska Press, 1997.

Olson, Wallace M. *The Tlingit: An Introduction to Their Culture and History*. Auke Bay, AK: Heritage Research, 1997.

Oberg, Kalervo. *The Social Economy of the Tlingit Indians*. Seattle: University of Washington Press, 1973.

Pelton, Mary Helen White and Jacqueline DiGennaro. *Images of a People: Tlingit Myths and Legends*. Englewood, CO: Libraries Unlimited, 1992.

Pritzker, Barry M. *Native Americans: an Encyclopedia of History, Culture, and Peoples*. Santa Barbara, CA: ABC-CLIO, 1998.

Swanton, John Reed. *Social Condition, Beliefs, and Linguistic Relationship of the Tlingit Indians*. Washington: Government Printing Office, 1908.

Swanton, John Reed. *Tlingit Myths and Texts*. Washington: Government Printing Office, 1909.

Wyatt, Victoria. *Images from the Inside Passage: An Alaskan Portrait by Winter & Pond*. Seattle: University of Washington Press in association with the Alaska State Library, Juneau, 1989.

Children's Books

The following books will be of interest to young people who would like to learn more about the Tlingit:

Boulé, Mary Null. *Northwest Coastal Region: Tlingit People*. Vashon, WA: Merryant Publishers, 1997.

Dixon, Ann. *How Raven Brought Light to People*. New York: M. K. McElderry Books, 1992.

Garza, Dolly A. *Tlingit Moon & Tide Teaching Resource: Elementary Level*. Fairbanks, AK: University of Alaska Sea Grant, 1999.

Martin, Nora. *The Eagle's Shadow*. New York: Scholastic Press, 1999.

Nichols, Richard. *A Story to Tell: Traditions of a Tlingit Community*. Minneapolis: Lerner Publications, 1998.

Staub, Frank J. *Children of the Tlingit*. Minneapolis, MN: Carolrhoda Books, 1999.

Wisniewski, David. *The Wave of the Sea-Wolf*. New York: Clarion Books, 1994.

Organizations

Alaska Inter-Tribal Council
431 W. 7th Ave., Suite 201
Anchorage, AK 99501
Phone: (907) 563-9334
Fax: (907) 563-9337

Alaska Native Heritage Center
8800 Heritage Center Drive
Anchorage, AK 99506
Phone: (907) 330-8000, (800) 315-6608
Fax: (907) 330-8030

Alaska State Museum
395 Whittier St.
Juneau, AK 99801-1718
Phone: (907) 465-2901
Fax: (907) 465-2976

Central Council Tlingit & Haida Indian Tribes of Alaska
320 W. Willoughby Ave., Suite 300
Juneau, AK 99801
Phone: (907) 463-7100, (800) 344-1432
Fax: (907) 586-8970

Sealaska Corporation
One Sealaska Plaza, Suite 400
Juneau, AK 99801-1276
Phone: (907) 586-1512
Fax: (907) 586-1826

Sheldon Jackson Museum
104 College Drive
Sitka, AK 99835-7657
Phone: (907) 747-8981
Fax: (907) 747-3004

Taku River Tlingit First Nation
(B.C./Yukon)
P.O. Box 132
Atlin, BC VOW lAO
Canada
Phone: (250) 651-7615
Fax: (250) 651-7714

Teslin Tlingit Council
P.O. Box 133
Teslin Yukon Territory YOA 1B0
Canada
Phone: (403) 390-2532 or 2204

Yakutat Tlingit Tribe

P.O. Box 418

Yakutat, AK 99689

Phone: (907) 784-3437

Fax: (907) 784-3556

Web Sites

Alaska Native Cultural Resources: Tlingit-Haida-Tsimshian
http://www.ankn.uaf.edu/southeast.html

Alaska Native Knowledge Network
http://www.ankn.uaf.edu/

Alaska Natives Online
http://members.aol.com/waya94/tlingit1.htm

Alaska State Museums
http://www.museums.state.ak.us/

Alaskan Tlingit and Tsimshian
http://content.lib.washington.edu/aipnw/miller1/index.html

Central Council Tlingit & Haida Indian Tribes of Alaska
http://www.tlingit-haida.org/

Kuiu Thlingit Nation—Kuiu Island, Alaska
http://www.geocities.com/CapitolHill/5803/

Raven's Window Alaskan Art from Haines
http://www.kcd.com/raven/

The Russian Church and Native Alaskan Cultures
http://lcweb.loc.gov/exhibits/russian/sla.html

Tlingit Culture

http://www.uidaho.edu/~ivie9341/tl_Nav4.html

Tlingit National Anthem

http://members.aol.com/waya94/page1.htm

The Tlingit of the Northwest Coast

http://www.carnegiemuseums.org/cmnh/exhibits/north-south-east-west/tlingit

Index

Page numbers for illustrations are in **boldface.**

Raymond Bial

HAS PUBLISHED MORE THAN THIRTY CRITICALLY ACCLAIMED BOOKS OF PHO-tographs for children and adults. His photo-essays for children include *Corn Belt Harvest, Amish Home, Frontier Home, Shaker Home, The Underground Railroad, Portrait of a Farm Family, With Needle and Thread: A Book About Quilts, Mist Over the Mountains: Appalachia and Its People, Cajun Home,* and *Where Lincoln Walked.*

He is currently immersed in writing *Lifeways,* a series of books about Native Americans. As with his other work, Bial's deep feeling for his subjects is evident in both the text and illustrations. He travels to tribal cultural centers, photographing homes, artifacts, and sur-roundings and learning firsthand about the national lifeways of these peoples.

A full-time library director at a small college in Champaign, Illinois, he lives with his wife and three children in nearby Urbana.